ALZHEIMER'S DISEASE

ALZHEIMER'S
DISEASE

BY ELAINE LANDAU

FRANKLIN WATTS
NEW YORK | LONDON | TORONTO | SYDNEY
A FIRST BOOK | 1987

Photographs courtesy of Mimi Forsyth, Monkmeyer Press:
pp. 14, 19, 39, 42, 44, 47, 52; David A. Weinstein,
courtesy of California Gardens Nursing Home
Compcare Services, Lincolnwood, Illinois:
pp. 17, 24, 27, 35, 40, 49, 53;
Stanley Rapoport, M.D.: pp. 31, 57;
National Institute of Health: p. 59.

Library of Congress Cataloging-in-Publication Data

Landau, Elaine.
Alzheimer's disease.

(A First book)
Bibliography: p.
Includes index.
Summary: Discusses this degenerative disease of
the nervous system, its effect on the patient's
family members, and suggestions for coping and care.
1. Alzheimer's disease—Juvenile literature.
[1. Alzheimer's disease] I. Title.
RC523.L36 1987   616.8'3   87-2095
ISBN 0-531-10376-5

CONTENTS

For my aunt and uncle,
Ida and Sidney Tudor,
and their grandchildren,
Katie and Matthew

ALZHEIMER'S DISEASE

CHAPTER

1

WHEN SOMEONE YOU KNOW HAS ALZHEIMER'S DISEASE

Imagine going out for a walk and being unable to return home because you forgot where you live. Or at times not recognizing your brother, sister, or best friend. Or wanting to say something important and being unable to find the right words.

This is just part of what victims of Alzheimer's disease must live with. Alzheimer's disease is a degenerative, progressive disease of the central nervous system. "Degenerative" means that the disease continues to worsen and the victims do not improve. It was first described in 1906 by a German medical specialist named Alois Alzheimer. At this time, there is no known cure for the disease. And no drugs have been discovered that can stop or reverse the effects of the disease.

Alzheimer's disease victims are generally over sixty-five years old. In the United States alone, two million adults have been affected. Today the disease is considered a major health problem. And as the number of older Americans continues to grow, the consequences of the disorder may become even more far-reaching.

In Alzheimer's disease, the victims' mind deteriorates first. They lose their memory and become confused. Many people can't find the right words to express themselves. Usually victims undergo disturbing personality changes. Then they will go into a physical decline that may take place over a six- to eight-year period.

During this time, the body slowly fails. Victims have trouble recognizing their surroundings or even dressing themselves. As time goes on, they will often be unable to walk or control their bodily functions. Although Alzheimer's disease is progressive, some patients have lingered on for as long as twenty years. Many die gradually, sinking into a coma and then death.

Several early warning signs are characteristic of the disorder. Among these are unusual changes in the person's thinking. For example, an experienced dressmaker will forget how to operate a sewing machine. Or an accountant will be unable to add numbers, even with a calculator. Anyone may be forgetful at times, but the changes in thinking brought on by Alzheimer's disease continue. There will be no general signs of improvement over the months. Instead, the victim's memory will continue to worsen.

During the early stages of the disease the patient may also undergo noticeable personality changes. People who used to be polite and gentle may now give way to emotional outbursts. Once soft-spoken people may be cross or harsh with others for no apparent reason. Alzheimer's disease victims often seem to be unusually nervous at times. They may weep uncontrollably or go into pointless rages.

In most cases, even before a doctor is called in, individuals suffering from Alzheimer's disease and their families usually sense that something is wrong. At times, they may brush aside these early warning signals or blame them on other factors. For example, they may attribute the unusual behavior and memory lapses to stress at work or family problems. For most people, the fear that something could be happening to their mind is extremely threatening. Victims of Alzheimer's, therefore, tend to deny that anything is wrong. Their refusal to recognize that a problem exists often causes them to put off getting medical help.

The case of a retired school secretary who didn't know she had Alzheimer's disease is a good example of this delaying tactic. At first, the woman enjoyed being called back to work occasionally when extra help was needed at the school. However, later she found it difficult to do her job. She often couldn't remember the principal's name. She also constantly mixed up the teachers' names as well as the subjects and grades they taught. She had always enjoyed working with young people, but now found herself spending more time disciplining the students than talking to them.

The secretary knew that something terrible was happening to her, yet she was unable to pinpoint the problem. Although later she admitted that she feared she was losing her mind, she tried not to think about it. Instead, she avoided the entire situation by refusing to return to work when asked.

However, she couldn't hide from the truth for too long, because her condition continued to grow worse. She found she couldn't remember even her grandchildren's names. At times, when she returned from shopping alone, she didn't recognize her own house.

Even then, the woman, claiming that nothing was wrong, refused her family's suggestion that she see a doctor. After a time, however, she gave in because she knew that she needed help. Her family promised that they would stand behind her regardless of the problem. Their support gave her the courage to look for answers.

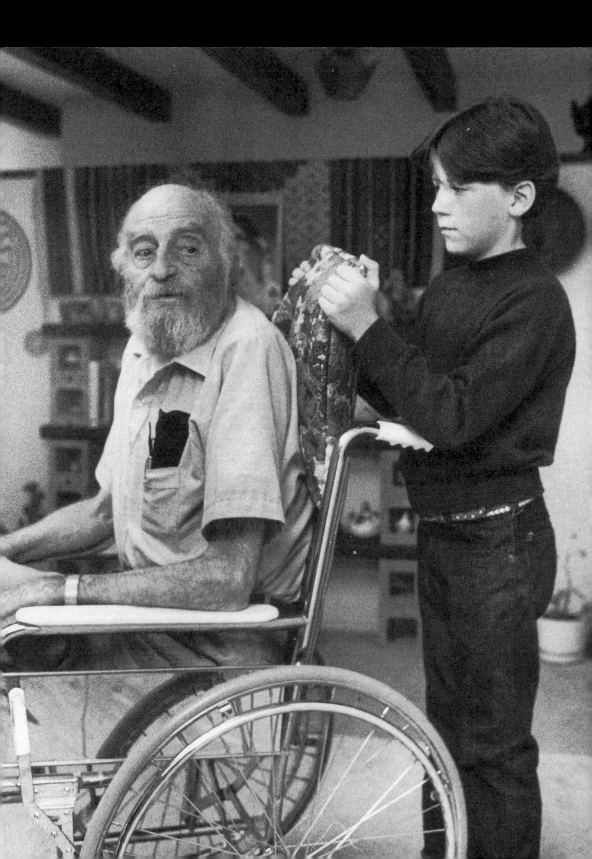

But the answers, when they come from a doctor and are not the ones the victim had hoped for, can be devastating. Learning that you have a progressive, incurable illness is not easy. Reactions to the diagnosis vary, depending on the person involved. But shock, anger, fear, and denial are common responses. This is how one sixty-seven-year-old man described his reaction to learning he had Alzheimer's disease:

I couldn't accept what I heard the doctors say. Somehow I expected a cure. Instead, I felt as though I had been handed a slow death sentence. The doctors and my family say that there's still much for me to enjoy in life. But I guess that it's easy enough for them to comfort me. After all, they aren't the ones who are losing their minds.

Some Alzheimer's disease victims are tremendously angry after their diagnosis. At times their rage may be directed at blameless family members. It is important for those people not to feel hurt or frightened by such reactions. They must try to understand what the ill person is going through and allow that person to vent his or her emotions. An Alzheimer's disease victim must adjust to a new and very painful reality.

Usually Alzheimer's disease affects not only the stricken individual, but that person's family as well. Often family members share in their relative's grief and loss. They may also be involved in that

A boy adjusts a cushion for his wheelchair-bound grandfather.

person's care as the disorder progresses. It is important for the family to learn exactly what the patient's future holds. New roles for various family members as well as available community resources in the area should be explored.

Generally, each family tends to deal with the issues surrounding Alzheimer's disease individually. Many doctors suggest that victims of Alzheimer's disease be informed of their condition—if they haven't been directly told—as soon as possible following the diagnosis. This enables patient and family to plan for the future together.

As one thirteen-year-old girl described her feelings:

Dealing with our grandmother's illness was difficult for everyone in our family. But I think that it was hardest for my younger sister, Beth. Beth had been named after Grandma. And she had always been our grandmother's favorite. I knew that Beth couldn't love Grandma any more than she did.

But over the past few months, our grandmother had changed. And the change was clearly for the worse. For example, one night Grandma called up our father and excitedly told him that our pastor had removed her blue living room sofa. She said that he had taken it to the church. Our father thought that this was highly unlikely. Nevertheless, he rushed over to grandmother's house. He hoped to calm her and to learn the facts. But as he opened the door, our father saw Grandma sitting on the very living room sofa that she claimed had been taken.

The list of our grandmother's unusual reactions seemed to grow daily. And after a time, Grandma was no longer able to live alone. So she moved in with us. But living with her wasn't easy. Some days she'd seem so normal; then she'd unexpectedly do something out of the ordinary.

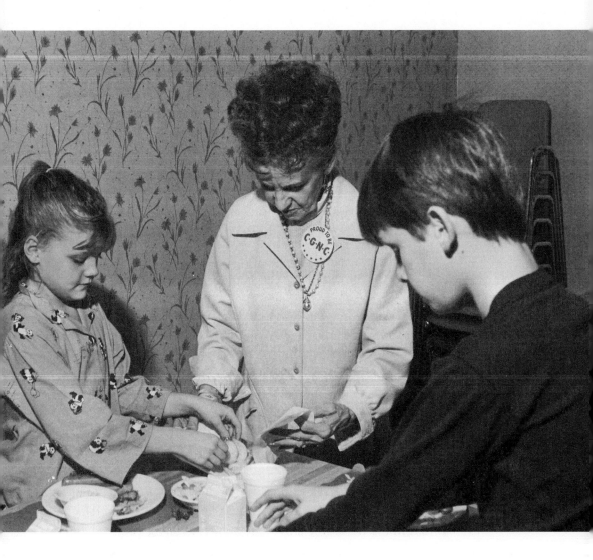

*Although a relative may have
Alzheimer's disease, family activities can
be shared and are good for the patient.*

Beth always still tried to include Grandma in our daily activities. My sister had her own small garden behind the backyard. Grandma seemed to enjoy watching Beth do the planting and weeding. Once Grandma asked if she could water the rows of tomatoes. Beth handed her the garden hose, only to watch Grandma aim it at a large tree at the garden's edge. Grandma just stood there, pointing the running hose at the tree's base. Beth was unable to stop her. Our father had to be called out to bring his mother back into the house.

As the months passed, our grandmother's condition placed an even greater strain on our family. Everyone was shocked when Grandma accused Mother of trying to poison her. She refused to allow Mother to cook for her any longer. Instead, Grandma insisted that Beth be the only one to prepare her food. And now she would only eat in the privacy of her own room.

Most of the time Mother continued to make Grandma's meals. Beth simply brought the tray up to her room. I knew that Grandmother still meant a great deal to Beth. She rarely refused any of Grandma's requests. Yet, I'll never forget the look on my sister's face one morning when she and I brought up our grandmother's breakfast tray. Grandma looked Beth straight in the face and said, "Well, hello, little girl, and who are you?"

Ill individuals appreciate the importance of taking care of legal and financial matters while their ability to think and reason is still intact. In this manner, Alzheimer's disease victims are also given a chance to help determine how they'll live out their remaining years.

Some patients who have been told their diagnosis still find it difficult to discuss their feelings. They may be afraid of upsetting other family members by dwelling on their illness. At times it may be helpful for those who are ill to confide in an understanding friend,

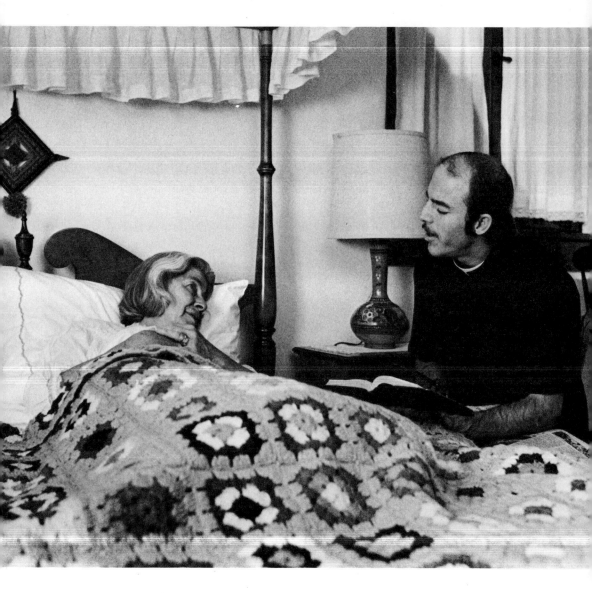

Clergymen can lend emotional support to Alzheimer's patients.

health professional, or member of the clergy. Usually there are many questions to be answered.

People with Alzheimer's disease may need reassurance to overcome their anxiety about the future. Many fear that they will be rejected by their family as they lose their ability to relate intelligently to others. It may be important for them to know that their family will support them.

Thinking lapses as well as speech and language problems resulting from the disorder often make communication difficult. For example, a family member may need to repeat an explanation to the patient a number of times. A twelve-year-old boy said this about his grandfather who had Alzheimer's disease:

When we heard that my grandfather had Alzheimer's disease, I wanted to help him. My mother said that we were all helpless in this situation. But she was wrong. As it turned out, there was a lot that I found I could do for him.

After my grandfather moved in with us, I sort of became his first mate. I learned to balance his checkbook. And I always went with him to the bank. Because of his illness, my grandfather now had trouble even with simple arithmetic.

Grandpa had lost most of his memory. So whenever we went to church or a family gathering, I'd make sure to stand near him. That way I could whisper people's names to him as they approached us. Before he died, my grandfather often said that I spared him a lot of embarrassment.

Some families in which a member has been stricken with this illness have found it helpful to try to make every moment count. An Alzheimer's disease victim does not become helpless overnight. Following an early diagnosis of the disease, the patient and his or her family will still have time to accomplish many family plans and goals.

The patient and family will be better able to cope by remaining optimistic about what can still be enjoyed. Family members should focus on what the patient can, rather than cannot, do.

CHAPTER

2

A FAMILY
AFFAIR

Alzheimer's disease often takes its toll on the victim's entire family. The Alzheimer's disease patient may have many physical, emotional, and social needs, and caring for that person can easily occupy much of the family's day.

Those who care for parents or relatives with Alzheimer's disease often feel torn between loyalty to the ill relative and their responsibility to other family members. In some cases, the patient's needs may become so overwhelming that the caregiver's life is greatly changed. Even long-established family routines are bound to be interrupted as the disorder worsens. Caring for a relative with a prolonged illness like this can make someone go through periods of alternating frustration, tenseness, anger, and sadness.

At first the patient may have been able to manage with little help. However, as the disorder progresses, the person becomes less and less able to plan activities or to complete even simple tasks. Eventually fulltime professional help may be necessary. Often in the final stages of the disorder, families find it too difficult to care for the patient at home.

The tasks involved in caring for an Alzheimer's disease victim may seem endless. If the family can afford it, it may be helpful for a home attendant to be hired. If outside help is not possible, it may be best for various family members to share caring for the ill person. When enough family members are available, duties can be rotated so that each person is given some time off.

Those who care for a relative with Alzheimer's disease must create a special balance in their lives. This is necessary so that other important family relationships can continue as well. Some health professionals have encouraged such families to meet together regularly. It is important to discuss the impact of their relative's illness on each of them. During such sessions, the rights of different family members versus the expected future needs of the patient may be discussed. In this manner, a family forum is created. Each individual's wishes are considered. The desired final outcome should represent as fairly as possible the best interests of both the patient and the other family members.

It is also essential that everyone involved with the patient emotionally accept the fact that Alzheimer's disease is a progressive and irreversible illness. The love and reassurance provided by family members may add to the patient's feelings of well-being. But no amount of care and attention can cure the patient. Loved ones who deny what will eventually happen may experience both anger and disappointment as their relative's condition worsens.

Caring for a person with diminishing mental capabilities can be especially frustrating. Dramatic personality changes may be extremely difficult to handle. A twenty-year-old woman described her grandmother's condition:

Alzheimer's disease can affect
all members of a family.

It's as if my grandmother is being taken from me bit by bit. Once when we were sitting in her den, my grandmother decided that we weren't at home. Instead, she thought that we were at the local bus depot. She kept asking me to take her home. I told her that we were already home. To convince her, I even walked my grandmother through all the rooms. But nothing helped. She pleaded to be taken home for the rest of the afternoon.

When I was married last June I wanted my grandmother to attend the ceremony. She had helped to raise me, and I didn't want her to be left out just because she had become ill. My grandmother attended the festivities, but we didn't have an easy time of it. She dressed for the ceremony in Bermuda shorts, a halter, and her old straw sunbonnet. It took over an hour and a half to persuade her to change. But even after she put on a dress, Grandmother came out to the car without her shoes.

At the reception my grandmother insisted on dancing alone in the ballroom. She also began to cut the wedding cake into tiny pieces before she could be stopped. I knew that the disease had caused her to behave that way. But it still hurt to share my wedding day with my grandmother in that way.

Unfortunately, there is still shame connected with mental disorders. Someone might openly say that a relative has cancer or heart disease. But that same person may not wish to admit that a member of his family can no longer think clearly. Often family members try to hide the fact that a relative has Alzheimer's disease. One sixty-two-year-old housewife told her story this way:

When my husband, Al, was diagnosed as having Alzheimer's disease, I knew that before long he would begin to act as though he were out of his mind. To shield him and our family from embarrassment, I tried to keep his illness a secret.

As Al worsened, it became harder to hide the truth. Friends noticed that my husband often slurred his speech and found it difficult to follow even a simple conversation. Our friends began to wonder if Al had a drinking problem.

Caring for Al by myself was extremely trying. He grew overly possessive of me. Al would complain or throw a temper tantrum if I as much as went out to the corner store or to the dry cleaners. Before long I realized that I had become a prisoner in my own jail. And now I found that I lacked the patience to properly care for my husband.

Eventually I revealed Al's problem to our friends. Everyone proved to be understanding and helpful. Sharing my feelings with others made me feel much better. And Al seemed to enjoy the company as well. Nothing could change what was happening to my husband, but it was wonderful not to be alone anymore.

Because Alzheimer's disease progresses gradually, both patients and their families must be prepared for continual changes in the ill person's daily activities. A person who is still working when diagnosed will probably not be able to continue working for very long. In fact, many Alzheimer's disease patients originally seek medical attention because they are experiencing problems at work.

How soon an Alzheimer's disease patient must stop working varies according to the individual. In some situations, a patient's safety may be at risk in the workplace once that person's judgment has been impaired. This may be especially true if the job involves driving a vehicle or operating complex machinery. Even if the patient's safety is not an issue, his or her inability to think clearly may make it impossible for the person to do the job properly.

A patient getting help with a computer

While the patient remains at home, some families have found it helpful to establish a daily routine. A planned schedule helps to keep the patient active. Most health professionals recommend that a patient be allowed to do as much as he or she is able to.

An individual who cannot complete household or gardening tasks may still be able to do a small portion of the work. For example, a person who is unable to mow a large lawn may still enjoy watering the flowers. At times the family may be unsure of what the patient can accomplish. In such instances, a psychological evaluation by a professional can be useful. These tests help to determine appropriate life and work roles for the ill family member.

Some physical exercise is important for Alzheimer's disease patients. Exercise often helps to reduce the need for sedatives. It also encourages a healthy appetite. For some, a short daily walk may be enough. Those who have been active in such sports as tennis, golf, swimming, or jogging should continue these activities for as long as they can. A familiar routine or activity helps to reinforce the patient's feelings of security. And participating in everyday activities gives the person a sense of accomplishment and self-esteem.

CHAPTER

3

MEDICAL QUESTIONS
AND ANSWERS ABOUT
ALZHEIMER'S DISEASE

1. What is the cause of
   Alzheimer's disease?

The cause is still unknown. One theory holds that Alzheimer's disease is caused by an infectious agent that acts very much like a virus. Other data suggest that the disease is caused by toxic agents in the environment such as aluminum. The cause of Alzheimer's disease may be quite complex, involving a number of factors that interact with one another.

2. Is Alzheimer's disease
   hereditary?

There may be a genetic factor involved in Alzheimer's disease. The disorder appears to run in some families. However, this has not been conclusively proven. The disease affects men and women almost equally. And its victims include people of all economic and social backgrounds.

3. How does someone know
   if he or she has
   Alzheimer's disease?

There is no single clinical test to identify the disease. Each person with possible Alzheimer's disease symptoms should undergo a number of procedures. The necessary laboratory procedures include blood studies, computerized tomography (CT scan), electroencephalography (EEG), and occasional studies of spinal fluid. Those procedures are used to determine whether other possible causes of the patient's symptoms exist, such as adverse reactions to drugs, tumors, nutritional deficiencies, and cardiovascular problems. On the basis of these tests and their observation of the patient, physicians may eliminate those other possibilities and arrive at a diagnosis of Alzheimer's disease. However, a true diagnosis of Alzheimer's disease can be confirmed only after the patient's death. This is because it requires looking at the patient's brain tissue. Such procedures are usually performed during an autopsy, which is an examination of the deceased person's body.

4. How does
   Alzheimer's disease
   affect the brain?

In Alzheimer's disease, specific changes occur within the brain. There is some shrinkage of the brain. There is also a loss of nerve cells in several areas of the brain considered necessary for effective thinking.

The brains of Alzheimer's disease patients contain widespread clusters of damaged nerve endings. These clusters are known as neu-

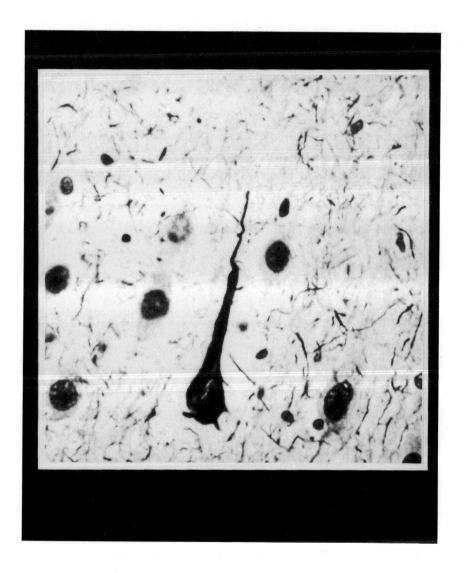

It is believed that neurofibrillary tangles interfere with normal nerve cell action.

ritic plaques. In addition, the brain contains a number of diseased neurons. Inside these diseased neurons are malformations known as neurofibrillary tangles. It is thought that the tangles interfere with normal cell action.

Alzheimer's disease also causes changes in the brain's neurotransmitters. Neurotransmitters are the chemical messengers with which nerve cells communicate. Alzheimer's disease especially affects one major neurotransmitter, known as acetylcholine. Acetylcholine is essential to memory. The disease affects other neurotransmitters in the brain as well.

5. What is dementia?

Dementia is the medical term that refers to serious disturbances in mental abilities. This includes the progressive loss of intellectual capacity. Although dementia may be brought on by a number of conditions, Alzheimer's is its most common cause.

Other conditions that cause dementia are frequently confused with Alzheimer's disease. Similar changes in intellect and behavior may also be brought on by a head injury, a brain tumor, a stroke, metabolic changes, poor nutrition, adverse drug reactions, liver or kidney disease, and other conditions. Psychiatric disorders are also often mistaken for dementia.

Although Alzheimer's disease cannot be halted or reversed, dementia caused by a number of other factors may be readily treatable. Therefore, a diagnosis of Alzheimer's disease must not be made until the patient has been thoroughly evaluated to eliminate any other possible causes of dementia.

CHAPTER

4

MEDICATION AND
THE PATIENT

Unfortunately, there are no known drugs that can stop or reverse the effects of Alzheimer's disease. However, there are medications that have been helpful in dealing with some aspects of the illness.

These drugs are known as psychotropic medications. They are generally used to alter emotions and problem behavior. Such medicines should be taken only under a doctor's supervision. The misuse of these drugs may serve to worsen symptoms. Psychotropic drugs can produce a wide range of unpleasant side effects in certain individuals. Therefore, patients must be carefully monitored while taking these drugs.

Drugs also tend to affect the older patient differently than a younger person. Aging alters the body structure so that it contains more fat and less protein. This increase in fatty tissue may influence the way in which the body handles some medications.

Some psychotropic drugs are drawn to the body's fatty tissue. This means that the drug is easily absorbed into body fat, leaving less medication available to travel to the brain or other areas of the body.

Medicines that tend to be stored in body fat also take longer to leave the body once the patient has stopped using the drug.

Older patients tend to metabolize or excrete drugs less efficiently than younger people. In some instances, very low doses of the drug must be prescribed to reduce the risk of unpleasant side effects.

The sensitivity of various parts of the body to different medicines also varies with age. The brain of an older person, especially someone with Alzheimer's disease, has been shown to be more sensitive to some drugs. Therefore, even mild amounts of such drugs may affect the patient powerfully.

It can be dangerous for someone with Alzheimer's disease to change the dosage of certain prescription drugs without his or her doctor's knowledge. Drinking alcoholic beverages can also be troublesome. Alcohol can alter how the body handles other drugs. Other negative side effects can occur as well.

Several types of psychotropic drugs may be used with Alzheimer's disease patients. Drugs known as antipsychotic medications lessen disturbing behavior. Violent reactions, restlessness, and hallucinations (seeing things that aren't there) tend to be reduced. Among the most common of these drugs are Thorazine®, Prolixin®, Navane®, Mellaril®, and Stelazine®.

Alzheimer's disease patients who are severely depressed may take psychotropic drugs known as antidepressants. Some of these are Elavil®, Norpramin®, and Tofranil®. Still other psychotropic drugs are sometimes prescribed by doctors to reduce anxiety. Such drugs, known as antianxiety medications, include Xanax®, Librium®, Tranxene®, Serax®, and Valium®. Some antianxiety medications may be habit-forming. Therefore, these drugs should never be taken routinely or for long periods. If patients are not carefully supervised, they can overdose on these drugs.

Bear in mind, however, that most physicians do not routinely use

Alzheimer's disease patients
should always consult a physician
before taking any medication.

drugs to treat depression, anxiety, or behavior problems in Alzheimer's disease patients. Each case is considered individually by the doctor involved.

For some patients, a change in environment can be helpful. Others may profit from counseling sessions. In some cases, time spent with reassuring family members and friends is the best medicine.

Many patients have trouble sleeping through the night. As their illness progresses, they may be awake and eager for activity at two or three o'clock in the morning. Many wander through the house at those odd hours. Sleep disturbances in these people have been extremely disruptive in many families. This behavior has often led families to place the patient in a nursing home.

Barbiturates and benzodiazepines are the two major classes of psychotropic drugs used to treat sleep disturbances. Most health professionals consider barbiturates a poor choice for older adults. Such drugs are addictive, can cause irritability in some patients, and may even worsen the sleep problems they are meant to eliminate.

Some physicians have prescribed benzodiazepines for Alzheimer's disease patients for limited periods of time. Among the most frequently used of these drugs are Noctec®, Mequin®, and Restoril®.

Sleep medications may cause other problems. At first, benzodiazepines may allow the patient to sleep through the night. However, he or she may appear increasingly drowsy and confused during the day. Many health professionals feel that sleep medications should be prescribed sparingly.

Changing the patient's routine may help to improve sleep habits. Rising at an early hour and skipping midday naps often prove to be beneficial. A proper diet, physical exercise, and interesting daily activities are also advisable. It may be unreasonable to expect an inactive person who has napped during the day to sleep comfortably through the night.

CHAPTER

5

COPING

At times, Alzheimer's disease becomes more than an illness. It can also be a label that brands the patient. Hearing that someone has Alzheimer's disease may immediately change the way in which others view as well as act toward that person. Someone may have difficulty thinking, working, reading, or speaking, but the person is still a human being. With Alzheimer's disease, the patient's abilities tend to decline at different rates. Although a person may develop many problem areas, other strengths may be present.

Sometimes even well-intentioned family members may not understand how the patient feels. They may incorrectly think that the person is completely unaware of what's going on around him or her. By taking over even the small tasks of which the patient is still capable, they may unintentionally make the patient feel helpless.

Even in the later stages of the illness, patients' beliefs, desires, and dreams may remain in spite of their illness.

Whenever possible, families should try to set aside special times to spend with the patient. The ill person will usually appreciate having an opportunity to express himself or herself. Family members will need to listen patiently. After a time many patients are unable to combine words into sentences. It may be hard for patients to make themselves understood. However, just listening to the patient will help him or her to feel more in touch with others.

As the disorder worsens, the patient may change the way he or she communicates as well. In the advanced stages of the illness, patients often depend more on body language and behavior changes than on words. Much of the anger and problem behavior seen in Alzheimer's disease victims are due to brain deterioration. However, at times such reactions may be the ill person's only way of showing his or her frustration at being unable to communicate.

Some people with this illness have waged their own personal battles against the disorder. Unfortunately, it's impossible to effectively combat brain deterioration. For example, one man who had started a successful family business was unable to accept the fact that he could no longer make even simple business decisions. His family had to force him to remain at home during the day.

As a result, the man suddenly became extremely short-tempered. He'd often scream or throw objects for no apparent reason. The man's two sons realized that their father was acting out of anger. He was enraged over having lost much of what he had been.

Fortunately, the sons were able to improve the situation. They arranged for their father to come into the office for a few hours each week to do simple things. Within weeks, the patient's outlook and behavior greatly improved.

Not every family can create a special workplace for an ill relative. However, there are many family activities that allow the patient to feel alive and vital. Playing with a child or pet, picking flowers, taking a walk, or watching television with other family members may be beneficial.

*An Alzheimer's patient talks things over
with a volunteer at a nursing home.*

Family support is extremely important for the patient.

One woman explained how she had resolved things with her mother:

Before her illness, my mother had always prided herself on being capable. She had raised five children while holding down a part-time job. As a young girl, I had thought that there wasn't anything my mother couldn't do if she set her mind to it.

After my mother was diagnosed as having Alzheimer's disease, everyone in our family tried to be helpful. My brothers and sisters and I wanted to show her how much she meant to us. But the more we did for her, the more upset our mother became. She wasn't able to easily accept our help. My mother had been used to being in charge. She wasn't comfortable in the role of patient.

I remember how on Thanksgiving she stood in the kitchen doorway watching my sister and me. We were busy preparing dinner for our eighteen guests. In the past, my mother had always made Thanksgiving dinner for all of us by herself. This was the first year that we had taken over.

Mother just watched us for a while. Then she gently asked if she could help. Intending to be kind, my sister told her that we didn't need any help. She suggested that Mother might enjoy watching television.

Hearing her words, Mother ran upstairs to her room. She locked the door and stayed there, crying for almost an hour. It was clear that she felt we had rejected her. When I tried to comfort her, Mother said, "It's over for me. I'm no more use to my family than a rag doll."

We began to find ways to make Mother feel useful again. She was no longer able to prepare a full meal by herself. However, she seemed delighted when we asked her to do simple things.

As her condition worsened, it became more difficult to include

Mother in many of our activities. But we had learned that making her feel needed was actually part of her care. And sometimes I thought it was the most important part.

The Alzheimer's disease patient should be allowed to do as much for himself or herself as possible. However, when assistance is necessary, it may be best to try to avoid using the word "help." Saying something like "Can we work on this together?" offers a sense of sharing rather than a feeling of helplessness to the ill person. The family should try to make the patient's life better in whatever small ways are possible. It is crucial that the patient not be regarded as invisible.

It is also important to find out whether any of the ill person's former activities are now harmful to his or her health or safety. A patient's wish to continue to drive a car can sometimes present a problem. Safe driving requires precise judgment, clear thinking, and quick reaction time. Good coordination is necessary too.

These skills diminish as the disorder advances. Although someone may know that he or she is ill, that person may not fully understand the extent of their losses. As a result, tempers may erupt as both family members and the patient argue their case.

For many people, driving represents a sense of freedom and independence. It may be difficult to suddenly have to depend on others for transportation. However, once a diagnosis of Alzheimer's disease has been made, the patient's ability to drive must be questioned. Not being permitted to drive may be upsetting to the patient, but with time its importance usually fades.

A patient enjoys creative art therapy.

Counseling for the Alzheimer's patient is sometimes helpful. The family's participation in a support group for the relatives of disease victims may prove valuable as well.

Family support groups are available through the Alzheimer's Disease and Related Disorders Association (ADRDA). Founded in 1980, ADRDA is a privately funded voluntary health organization. The group does a great deal to assist Alzheimer's disease victims and their families. There are 159 ADRA chapters and over 1,000 support groups in cities across the country.

According to Jerome Stern, president of the board of directors of ADRDA, "Many members of local ADRDA organizations are personally affected by a spouse or family member suffering from Alzheimer's. They have a special sensitivity to the needs of others trying to cope with the disease."

Family support can range from suggestions for patient care at home to referrals to other nursing programs. Support groups are run by health care professionals and experienced caregivers. These groups meet on a regular basis. People share information as well as find answers to questions. They act as the sympathetic ear to Alzheimer's families faced with what has been called "the thirty-six-hour day."

For further information on these groups as well as other resources available to Alzheimer's disease patients and their families, call ADRDA at the following toll-free numbers: 800-621-0379; in Illinois, call 800-572-6037.

Trying to maintain some
degree of normal life is
important for disease victims.

CHAPTER

6

NURSING HOME
CARE

Each year thousands of families make the decision to place a relative in a nursing home. For many, this choice may be a difficult one. In some cases, a nursing home might provide the best available care for the patient. Still, entering one may be viewed as a tragic end. Family members may experience a sense of guilt. They may feel as though they've failed their ill relative by not being able to care for him or her at home.

However, in many instances, nursing home care may be superior to the level of care that could be provided at home. Extended home care is not a workable alternative for everyone. In families in which all the adults work, the cost of hiring someone to remain at home with the patient may be too high. Leaving the patient unsupervised during the day might be dangerous for the person. In instances where the patient's health is poor, continuous nursing care may be required.

People who are unmanageable or exhibit violent behavior may not be good candidates for home care either.

Nursing homes can provide the support
and expert care many patients need.

One woman described her decision to find a nursing home for her mother this way:

On the night I learned that my mother had Alzheimer's disease, I promised myself that I would never place her in a nursing home. That was in the early stages of my mother's disorder, before I had any idea of how bad things could become.

At first my mother really wasn't all that different. She just seemed to have memory lapses and difficulty speaking. But as the months passed, my mother changed in unimaginable ways.

At times we feared for her safety. She began to wander out of the house a great deal. This presented serious problems. After leaving the house, she'd forget how to return. Once our minister found her sitting on a curb a few blocks away. She was lost and crying.

I tried to tell my mother not to go out alone. But she wasn't capable of understanding what I meant. So I tried to always have someone with her. But the moment we'd turn our backs, Mother was out the door.

My mother also had trouble sleeping. As her illness worsened, she spent most nights roaming around the house. But her waking up in the middle of the night wasn't the worst of it. Sometimes Mother would leave the house after midnight. Even in cold weather, she would wander out in her nightgown, without slippers. One night she left the house in her slip.

Health-care professionals can play a significant role in the care of Alzheimer's patients.

—48—

I was concerned about my mother's welfare. After a while I couldn't sleep soundly myself. I always tried to be on the alert. That way if my mother woke up, I could guide her back to bed.

But my mother continued to risk her safety in other ways as well. She constantly confused the oven with the pantry cabinets. Once she put a package of cereal, a container of salt, and three boxes of Jello in the oven. Then she turned the knob to broil. Another time she placed a magazine in an empty pot on the stove and turned the gas burner on.

I smelled the burning pot upstairs in my sewing room. But when I rushed to the kitchen and asked Mother what she was doing, she just stared at me in disbelief. She said she didn't know why I was so upset. Couldn't I see that she was only cooking up a pot of applesauce? Wasn't that my favorite dessert?

After about a year, my mother's behavior began to disturb our entire family. At first I didn't want to believe it, but my mother was becoming violent and abusive towards others. She would fly into a rage over the slightest incident. She had become quick to scream at other family members. As I listened to her, it was hard to believe that I was actually hearing my own mother. She had been so pleasant and soft-spoken before her illness.

It was about this time that Mother became extremely possessive of me as well. She tried to never let me out of her sight. She even wanted to follow me into the bathroom. One night she simply walked into my bedroom and ordered my husband to go to the den and stay there. Mother had decided that she wanted to watch television alone with me.

One Saturday my mother even threw an ashtray at my thirteen-year-old daughter. I guess that she had become jealous. I had spent the entire afternoon helping my daughter with her part in the school play. Fortunately, Mother's aim was poor. The ashtray fell to the floor, having missed my child. By now Mother had come to demand all my attention. She was unable to accept that there were others in my life.

I still loved my mother in spite of the problems she caused. I knew that she couldn't help what was happening to her. Her behavior was a direct result of her illness. Yet I knew that she couldn't live with us for very much longer.

I worried about my children. I knew that I had an obligation to the other people I loved as well. What Alzheimer's disease has done to my mother was terrible enough. I couldn't allow it to destroy all of us.

And the night I found her chasing my seven-year-old son through the house with a fly swatter, I knew what I had to do. At this point we were unable to handle my mother at home. I'd have to look for a nursing home for her.

Families should not feel they are betraying their sick relative by placing the person in a nursing home. The nursing home may simply be a better health-care choice. Many nursing homes are physically designed to best meet the needs of older patients. Activities and programs suitable for people with restricted physical and mental capabilities are available as well. Such facilities may also offer group and individual counseling sessions for the residents.

Whenever possible, families should allow enough planning time to find the best home for their relative. Nursing homes tend to vary greatly in quality. Entering a nursing home should be discussed with the ill person before the actual move. In some cases, the patient's condition may have worsened to the point where he or she cannot actively take part in the discussion. Nevertheless, that person should still be present.

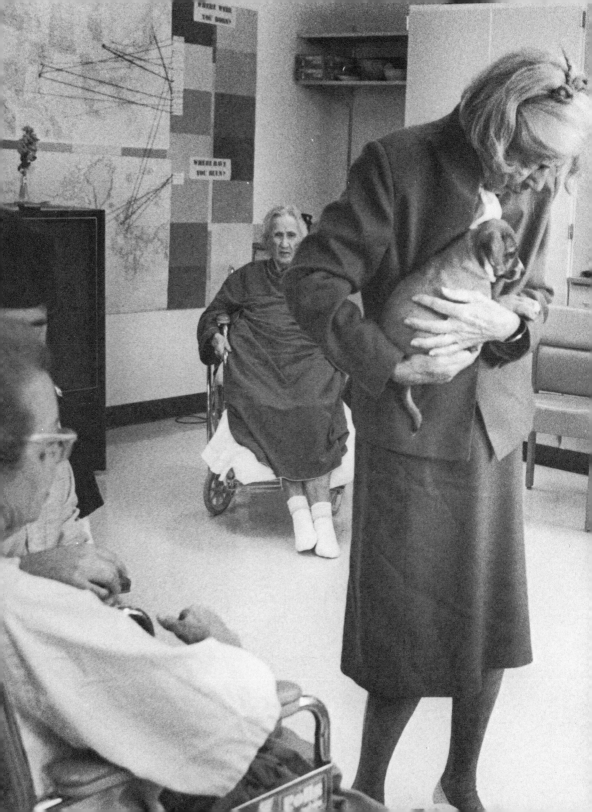

Above: *the friendship and concern*
of other disease victims can be
of great comfort to a patient.
Left: *at times the love of an animal*
is a great help to sick people.

CHAPTER

7

PARTING

I don't think I'll ever forget the day my great-aunt died. She'd been living with us for about two years at the time of her death. She had become very frail and prone to illness during the last six months of her life. But somehow I still thought that Aunt Hilda was going to live forever.

She'd been a part of my life for as long as I could remember. And I couldn't picture my life without her. My parents had warned me that I'd have to, but I refused to think about it. My great-aunt had Alzheimer's disease.

Aunt Hilda died on the Sunday that my cousin Peter turned sixteen. We had a family party for him that afternoon. Before he left, Peter wanted to say good-bye to Aunt Hilda. She was napping in her room, but my mother told Peter to wake her. My mother thought that Aunt Hilda would enjoy seeing him.

Peter returned alone a few minutes later. He looked upset. He walked over to my mother and whispered to her that he had been unable to wake Aunt Hilda. My mother rushed into my great-aunt's room. She came out sobbing. The local emergency service was called. The medics confirmed what by now had become obvious. Aunt Hilda was dead.

Before her body was taken from our house, my mother asked if I wanted to go in and say good-bye to Aunt Hilda. I tried to, but I couldn't get past the doorway. Aunt Hilda was still lying in her bed. She didn't look dead, or at least the way I thought that a dead person would look. Her eyes were open and her face seemed peaceful.

I ran from her room down to the basement. I crawled into this small space between the washer and dryer in our laundry room. As a very young child, I used to hide there when I didn't want anyone to find me. But Aunt Hilda always knew where I was. She used to come downstairs with a plate of fudge and a smile to make things better.

And as I sat crying in my special place that Sunday, I had to face the fact that my great-aunt was never going to come down those basement stairs again.

It's always painful to have someone we love die, even if we know that the person is suffering from an incurable disorder. Grieving and accepting the loss take time. It is not unnatural to mourn for someone who meant a great deal to us. Although it may seem as though the pain will never go away, it will.

Grief differs among individuals and families. The death of a close relative may spark a broad range of feelings. Sadness, pain, anger, and even guilt may all be experienced at different times. There is no one correct way to mourn or to accept the loss of someone who has been close to you. But it's important that surviving family members be able to openly express their feelings about what has happened.

The death of an Alzheimer's disease patient may be especially difficult for family members. Alzheimer's disease has been described by countless families as a slow death of sorts. As their relative's brain deterioration progresses, they continue to gradually lose much of that person. They may have begun to adjust to their relative's fate, but the patient's actual death is still usually a shock. The loss of someone we love can be difficult even if we think we are prepared for it.

When a patient dies of Alzheimer's disease, the doctor involved may ask the family's permission to perform an autopsy. An autopsy is a clinical examination of a body following death. If the family has been part of a support group for the relatives of Alzheimer's disease victims, they may also be urged by researchers who have visited their group to have an autopsy performed.

Postmortem examinations, or autopsy studies, have helped researchers learn a great deal about the brain. This is especially true in the case of Alzheimer's disease. With this disease, the brain cells deteriorate at different rates. Researchers hope that if one day the cause of this cell deterioration is discovered, they may be able to develop a drug to stop or even reverse the process.

The present research outlook is hopeful as several important new discoveries have recently been made. Some promising results were announced by biochemist Peter Davies of New York City's Albert Einstein College of Medicine in 1986. Davies and his graduate assistant Benjamin Wolozin identified an abnormal protein in the brains of Alzheimer's disease victims.

The protein is called A-68. A-68 also appears in the spinal fluid of living patients thought to have the disease. At this time, it is not known if A-68 plays a role in causing Alzheimer's disease, but the discovery and isolation of the A-68 protein opens the possibility of developing a routine laboratory test to detect Alzheimer's disease.

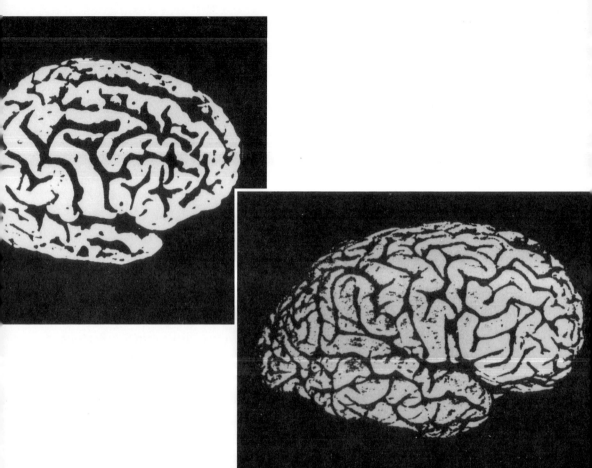

A comparison of a brain
with Alzheimer's disease
(left) and a normal brain

The findings of other ongoing experiments conducted throughout 1986-87 by Dr. Dmitry Goldgaber and his associates from the National Institute of Neurological and Communicative Disorders and Stroke (NINCDS) revealed the possibility that Alzheimer's disease may either be caused or activated by a defective human gene. The gene, which is located on chromosome 21, is also thought to produce the protein A-68.

Additional work is being done to develop new drugs to inhibit some of the symptoms associated with the disease. One such experimental drug is known as tetrahydroaminoacridine (THA). Although THA may relieve some of the discomfort experienced by Alzheimer's disease victims, the drug is not considered a cure for the disease.

Advances such as these may prove to be extremely beneficial to those suffering from Alzheimer's. An early diagnosis of the disorder and the lessening or delay of symptoms as well as an eventual cure may all be on the research horizon. However, at this time, scientists stress that they still have much to learn about Alzheimer's disease. A considerable amount of work will be needed to allow them to determine exactly what it is they are up against.

Brain autopsies are necessary to achieve that goal. The Alzheimer's Disease and Related Disorders Association (ADRDA) has actively supported the development of brain banks in the United States. Such banks allow for the availability and proper storage of brain tissue needed for medical research.

Some families discuss the possibility of an autopsy with the patient in the early stages of the disorder. A doctor or member of the clergy may be involved in these discussions. Some patients may agree to the autopsy and sign the consent forms. Some want time to

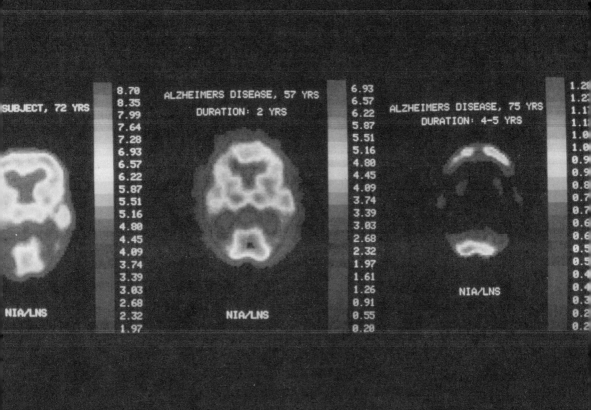

SUBJECT, 72 YRS

8.70
8.35
7.99
7.64
7.28
6.93
6.57
6.22
5.87
5.51
5.16
4.80
4.45
4.09
3.74
3.39
3.03
2.68
2.32
1.97

NIA/LNS

ALZHEIMERS DISEASE, 57 YRS
DURATION: 2 YRS

6.93
6.57
6.22
5.87
5.51
5.16
4.80
4.45
4.09
3.74
3.39
3.03
2.68
2.32
1.97
1.61
1.26
0.91
0.55
0.20

NIA/LNS

ALZHEIMERS DISEASE, 75 YRS
DURATION: 4-5 YRS

1.2
1.2
1.1
1.1
1.0
1.0
0.9
0.9
0.8
0.7
0.7
0.6
0.6
0.5
0.5
0.4
0.4
0.3
0.2
0.2

NIA/LNS

A CAT-scan compares a normal brain with two diseased brains at different stages of deterioration.

think about it. Others reject the procedure. Some patients refuse because their religious beliefs prohibit autopsies. The autopsy question should be discussed whenever possible while the patient is still able to make rational decisions. In such cases, the decision belongs solely to the patient.

Some families are not able to discuss the possibility of an autopsy with the patient because they might find it too painful. Those people will usually have to make the decision themselves in the final stage of their relative's illness. In such instances, it is often best to have several family members take part in the decision.

Whether or not an autopsy should be performed is a highly personal matter. Some people choose that option because they believe that their deceased relative would want to help prevent others from suffering. Families often feel an autopsy allows the former patient to live on in the sense that he or she is still making a valuable contribution to society.

Autopsies play a significant part in the research done on Alzheimer's disease. However, the decision of whether or not one should be performed is just a small part of what surviving family members of an Alzheimer's disease patient must face. Each person must learn to face and deal with the loss. One fifteen-year-old girl described her experience:

Every Friday after school, I used to meet my mother at my grandmother's nursing home. I went there directly from school because it was only a few blocks from my junior high. My mother and grandmother were always sitting out on the porch waiting to greet me.

But one Friday when I arrived, they were nowhere in sight. I went into the building and found a nurse I recognized. I asked her if she'd seen my mother. The nurse told me that my mother was having a conference with the nursing home director in his office. She asked me to wait in the lobby.

I didn't want to wait. I was anxious to see my grandmother. So I told her that instead I'd go down to my grandmother's room and spend some time with her. She tried to stop me, but I guess I was too quick for her. My grandmother's room was only two doors away. I sprinted down the hall and flung the door open.

As I looked around the room, it was as if someone had just dropped a hundred-pound stone to the pit of my stomach. The room had been stripped bare. All my grandmother's perfumes, combs, and brushes had been removed from her dresser. Her housecoat and slippers had been taken from the windowseat. The quilt that covered the seat of her rocking chair was gone, and the bed had been stripped of the sheets and her down comforter. Now only a thin gray and black striped mattress lay on top of the slim iron bed frame.

At that point nobody needed to tell me what had happened. I knew that my grandmother was gone too. She must have died earlier that day while I was still in school. I sat down on the mattress and began to cry. I kept thinking how I didn't get to say good-bye.

The nurse I spoke to earlier had followed me into the room. She sat down beside me and put her arms around me. She asked me if I wanted to talk, but I said that there was nothing to talk about. My grandmother was dead. She was gone and that was that.

The nurse smiled at me and, while still holding me close, suggested something that I'll never forget. She said, "You know, your grandmother may be dead, but I don't think of her as gone. I see her sweetness in your smile and your caring. A part of her continues to live on in the best part of you. Your challenge is to let your grandmother's real legacy survive through all the good things you achieve."

It's now been about six months since my grandmother's death. I often think about what that nurse said. And every time I do something extra for someone, I say to myself, "That's Grandma in me." Sharing my life with her helped to make me who I am now. And nothing can ever take that away. Not even Alzheimer's disease.

BIBLIOGRAPHY

Alzheimer's Disease and Related Disorders Association. *Understanding Alzheimer's Disease.* New York: Scribner, 1985.

Brown, Dorothy. *Handle with Care: A Question of Alzheimer's.* Buffalo, N.Y.: Prometheus Books, 1985.

Cohen, Donna, and Carl Eisdorfer. *The Loss of Self.* New York: W. W. Norton, 1986.

Frank, Julia, *Alzheimer's Disease: The Silent Epidemic.* Minneapolis, Minn: Lerner Publications, 1985.

Heston, Leonard, and June White. *Dementia: A Practical Guide for Alzheimer's Disease and Related Illnesses.* New York: W. H. Freeman, 1983.

Holland, Gail B. *For Sasha with Love: An Alzheimer's Crusade: The Anne Bashkiroff Story.* New York: Dembner Books, 1985.

Mace, Nancy, and Peter Rabins. *The 36-Hour Day.* New York: Warner Books, 1984.

Powell, Lenore, and Katie Courtice. *Alzheimer's Disease: A Guide for Families.* Reading, Mass: Addison-Wesley, 1983.

Reisberg, Barry. *A Guide to Alzheimer's Disease: For Families, Spouses, and Friends.* New York: Free Press, 1984.

Roach, Marion. *Another Name for Madness.* Boston: Houghton Mifflin, 1985.

INDEX

ABOUT THE AUTHOR

Elaine Landau received a bachelor's degree
in English and Journalism from
New York University and a master's degree
in Library and Information Science
from Pratt Institute.

She has worked as a newspaper reporter,
an editor, and a librarian, but
she especially enjoys researching
and writing books on contemporary issues
for young readers.

Ms. Landau makes her home in New York City.